AN ANTHOLOGY OF
Favourite Poems

ILLUSTRATED WITH PHOTOGRAPHS FROM
THE FRANCIS FRITH COLLECTION

Chosen and edited by
Terence and Eliza Sackett

First published in the United Kingdom in 2003 by
Black Horse Books (an imprint of the Frith Book Company)

This revised and updated edition published by the
Frith Book Company in 2005

British Library Cataloguing in Publication Data
An Anthology of Favourite Poems
Chosen and edited by Terence and Eliza Sackett
ISBN 1-84589-000-0

Although the publishers have tried to contact all copyright holders before
publication, this has not proved possible in every case. If notified, the
publisher will be pleased to make any necessary arrangements.

Frith Book Company
Frith's Barn, Teffont,
Salisbury, Wiltshire SP3 5QP
Tel: +44 (0) 1722 716 376
Email: info@francisfrith.co.uk
www.francisfrith.co.uk

Cover Image: **MILFORD**, Farming c1955 M76060p

The colour-tinting is for illustrative purposes only, and is not intended to be historically accurate

Printed and bound in England

Contents

Pippa's Song

THE year's at the spring,
And day's at the morn;
Morning's at seven;
The hill-side's dew-pearled;
The lark's on the wing;
The snail's on the thorn:
God's in His heaven—
All's right with the world!

ROBERT BROWNING (1812-1889)
from Pippa Passes

Spring, the Sweet Spring

SPRING, the sweet spring, is the year's pleasant king;
Then blooms each thing, then maids dance in a ring,
Cold doth not sting, the pretty birds do sing—
Cuckoo, jug-jug, pu-we, to-witta-woo!

The palm and may make country houses gay,
Lambs frisk and play, the shepherds pipe all day,
And we hear aye birds tune this merry lay—
Cuckoo, jug-jug, pu-we, to-witta-woo!

The fields breathe sweet, the daisies kiss our feet,
Young lovers meet, old wives a-sunning sit,
In every street these tunes our ears do greet—
Cuckoo, jug-jug, pu-we, to-witta-woo!
Spring, the sweet spring!

THOMAS NASHE (1567-1601)

The Cuckoo

O THE cuckoo she's a pretty bird,
She singeth as she flies,
She bringeth good tidings,
She telleth no lies.

She sucketh white flowers
For to keep her voice clear,
And the more she singeth cuckoo
The summer draweth near.

ANON

from The Daffodils

I WANDERED lonely as a cloud
That floats on high o'er vales and hills,
When all at once I saw a crowd,
A host, of golden daffodils,
Beside the lake, beneath the trees,
Fluttering and dancing in the breeze …

The waves beside them danced, but they
Out-did the sparkling waves in glee:
A poet could not but be gay
In such a jocund company!
I gazed—and gazed—but little thought
What wealth the show to me had brought:

For oft, when on my couch I lie
In vacant or in pensive mood,
They flash upon that inward eye
Which is the bliss of solitude;
And then my heart with pleasure fills,
And dances with the daffodils.

WILLIAM WORDSWORTH (1770-1850)

I Bended Unto Me a Bough of May

I BENDED unto me a bough of May,
That I might see and smell:
It bore it in a sort of way,
It bore it very well.
But when I let it backward sway,
Then it were hard to tell

With what a toss, with what a swing,
The dainty thing
Resumed its proper level,
And sent me to the devil.
I know it did—you doubt it?
I turned, and saw them whispering about it.

T E BROWN (1830-1897)

from The Question

I DREAMED that as I wandered by the way
Bare Winter suddenly was changed to Spring,
And gentle odours led my steps astray,
Mixed with a sound of waters murmuring
Along a shelving bank of turf, which lay
Under a copse, and hardly dared to fling
Its green arms round the bosom of the stream,
But kissed it and then fled, as thou mightest in dream.

There grew pied wind-flowers and violets,
Daisies, those pearled Arcturi of the earth,
The constellated flower that never sets;
Faint oxlips; tender blue-bells, at whose birth
The sod scarce heaved; and that tall flower that wets—
Like a child, half in tenderness and mirth—
Its mother's face with heaven's collected tears
When the low wind, its playmate's voice, it hears …

Methought that of these visionary flowers
I made a nosegay, bound in such a way
That the same hues, which in their natural bowers
Were mingled or opposed, the like array
Kept these imprisoned children of the Hours
Within my hand;—and then, elate and gay,
I hastened to the spot whence I had come,
That I might there present it—O! to whom?

PERCY BYSSHE SHELLEY (1792-1822)

from Ode to a Nightingale

MY HEART aches, and a drowsy numbness pains
My sense, as though of hemlock I had drunk,
Or emptied some dull opiate to the drains
One minute past, and Lethe-wards had sunk:
'Tis not through envy of thy happy lot,
But being too happy in thine happiness,—
That thou, light-winged Dryad of the trees,
In some melodious plot
Of beechen green, and shadows numberless,
Singest of summer in full-throated ease …

I cannot see what flowers are at my feet,
Nor what soft incense hangs upon the boughs,
But, in embalmed darkness, guess each sweet
Wherewith the seasonable month endows
The grass, the thicket, and the fruit-tree wild;
White hawthorn, and the pastoral eglantine;
Fast-fading violets covered up in leaves;
And mid-May's eldest child
The coming musk-rose, full of dewy wine,
The murmurous haunt of flies on summer eves.

Darkling I listen; and, for many a time
I have been half in love with easeful Death,
Called him soft names in many a mused rhyme,
To take into the air my quiet breath;
Now more than ever seems it rich to die,

To cease upon the midnight with no pain,
While thou art pouring forth thy soul abroad
In such an ecstasy!
Still wouldst thou sing, and I have ears in vain—
To thy high requiem become a sod.

Thou wast not born for death, immortal Bird!
No hungry generations tread thee down;
The voice I hear this passing night was heard
In ancient days by emperor and clown:
Perhaps the self-same song that found a path
Through the sad heart of Ruth, when, sick for home,
She stood in tears amid the alien corn;
The same that oft-times hath
Charmed magic casements, opening on the foam
Of perilous seas, in faery lands forlorn.

Forlorn! the very word is like a bell
To toll me back from thee to my sole self!
Adieu! the fancy cannot cheat so well
As she is famed to do, deceiving elf.
Adieu! adieu! thy plaintive anthem fades
Past the near meadows, over the still stream,
Up the hill-side; and now 'tis buried deep
 In the next valley-glades:
Was it a vision, or a waking dream?
Fled is that music:—Do I wake or sleep?

JOHN KEATS (1795-1821)

Adlestrop

YES, I remember Adlestrop—
The name, because one afternoon
Of heat the express-train drew up there
Unwontedly. It was late June.

The steam hissed. Someone cleared his
throat.
No one left and no one came
On the bare platform. What I saw
Was Adlestrop—only the name

And willows, willow-herb, and grass,
And meadowsweet, and haycocks dry,
No whit less still and lonely fair
Than the high cloudlets in the sky.

And for that minute a blackbird sang
Close by, and round him, mistier,
Farther and farther, all the birds
Of Oxfordshire and Gloucestershire.

EDWARD THOMAS (1878-1917)

To Autumn

SEASON of mists and mellow fruitfulness,
Close bosom-friend of the maturing sun;
Conspiring with him how to load and bless
With fruit the vines that round the thatch-eves run;
To bend with apples the mossed cottage-trees,
And fill all fruit with ripeness to the core;
To swell the gourd, and plump the hazel shells
With a sweet kernel; to set budding more,
And still more, later flowers for the bees,
Until they think warm days will never cease,
For Summer has o'er-brimmed their clammy cells.

Who hath not seen thee oft amid thy store?
Sometimes whoever seeks abroad may find
Thee sitting careless on a granary floor,
Thy hair soft-lifted by the winnowing wind;
Or on a half-reaped furrow sound asleep,
Drowsed with the fume of poppies, while thy hook
Spares the next swath and all its twined flowers;
And sometimes like a gleaner thou dost keep
Steady thy laden head across a brook;
Or by a cider-press, with patient look,
Thou watchest the last oozings, hours by hours.

Where are the songs of Spring? Ay, where are they?
Think not of them,—thou hast thy music too,
While barred clouds bloom the soft-dying day
And touch the stubble-plains with rosy hue;
Then in a wailful choir the small gnats mourn
Among the river sallows, borne aloft
Or sinking as the light wind lives or dies;
And full-grown lambs loud bleat from hilly
bourn;
Hedge-crickets sing, and now with treble soft
The redbreast whistles from a garden-croft,
And gathering swallows twitter in the skies.

JOHN KEATS (1795-1821)

Blow, Blow, Thou Winter Wind

BLOW, blow, thou winter wind,
Thou art not so unkind
As man's ingratitude;
Thy tooth is not so keen
Because thou art not seen,
Although thy breath be rude.
Heigh ho! sing, heigh ho! unto the green holly:
Most friendship is feigning, most loving mere folly:
Then, heigh ho! the holly!
This life is most jolly.

Freeze, freeze, thou bitter sky,
That dost not bite so nigh
As benefits forgot:
Though thou the waters warp,
Thy sting is not so sharp
As friend remembered not.
Heigh ho! sing, heigh ho! unto the green holly:
Most friendship is feigning, most loving mere folly:
Then, heigh ho, the holly!
This life is most jolly.

WILLIAM SHAKESPEARE (1564-1616)
from As You Like It

from Ode to the North-East Wind

WELCOME, wild North-easter!
Shame it is to see
Odes to every zephyr;
Ne'er a verse to thee.
Welcome, black North-easter!
O'er the German foam;
O'er the Danish moorlands,
From thy frozen home.
Tired we are of summer,
Tired of gaudy glare,
Showers soft and steaming,
Hot and breathless air.
Tired of listless dreaming,
Through the lazy day:
Jovial wind of winter,
Turn us out to play!
Sweep the golden reed-beds;
Crisp the lazy dike;
Hunger into madness
Every plunging pike.
Fill the lake with wild-fowl;
Fill the marsh with snipe;
While on dreary moorlands
Lonely curlew pipe.
Through the black fir-forest
Thunder harsh and dry,
Shattering down the snow-flakes

Off the curdled sky …
Let the luscious South-wind
Breathe in lovers' sighs,
While the lazy gallants
Bask in ladies' eyes.
What does he but soften
Heart alike and pen?
'Tis the hard gray weather
Breeds hard English men.
What's the soft South-wester?
'Tis the ladies' breeze,
Bringing home their trueloves
Out of all the seas:
But the black North-easter,
Through the snow-storm hurled,
Drives our English hearts of oak
Seaward round the world.
Come, as came our fathers,
Heralded by thee,
Conquering from the eastward,
Lords by land and sea.
Come; and strong within us
Stir the Vikings' blood;
Bracing brain and sinew;
Blow, thou wind of God!

CHARLES KINGSLEY (1819-1875)

The Beasts

I THINK I could turn and live with animals,
they are so placid and self-contained;
I stand and look at them long and long.
They do not sweat and whine about their condition;
They do not lie awake in the dark and weep for their sins;
They do not make me sick discussing their duty to God;
Not one is dissatisfied—not one is demented with the
mania of owning things;
Not one kneels to another, nor to his kind that lived
thousands of years ago;
Not one is respectable or industrious over the whole earth.

WALT WHITMAN (1819-1892)
from Leaves of Grass

Milk for the Cat

WHEN the tea is brought at five o'clock,
And all the neat curtains are drawn with care,
The little black cat with bright green eyes
Is suddenly purring there.

At first she pretends, having nothing to do,
She has come in merely to blink by the grate,
But, though tea may be late or the milk may be sour,
She is never late.

And presently her agate eyes
Take a soft large milky haze,
And her independent casual glance
Becomes a stiff, hard gaze.

Then she stamps her claws or lifts her ears,
Or twists her tail and begins to stir,
Till suddenly all her lithe body becomes
One breathing, trembling purr.

The children eat and wriggle and laugh;
The two old ladies stroke their silk:
But the cat is grown small and thin with desire,
Transformed to a creeping lust for milk.

The white saucer like some full moon descends

At last from the clouds of the table above;
She sighs and dreams and thrills and glows,
Transfigured with love.
She nestles over the shining rim,

Buries her chin in the creamy sea;
Her tail hangs loose; each drowsy paw
Is doubled under each bending knee.

A long, dim ecstasy holds her life;
Her world is an infinite shapeless white,
Till her tongue has curled the last holy drop,
Then she sinks back into the night,

Draws and dips her body to heap
Her sleepy nerves in the great arm-chair,
Lies defeated and buried deep
Three or four hours unconscious there.

HAROLD MONRO (1879-1932)

On a Favourite Cat, Drowned in a Tub of Goldfishes

'TWAS on a lofty vase's side,
Where China's gayest art had dyed
The azure flowers that blow;
Demurest of the tabby kind,
The pensive Selima, reclined,
Gazed on the lake below.

Her conscious tail her joy declared:
The fair round face, the snowy beard,
The velvet of her paws,
Her coat that with the tortoise vies,
Her ears of jet, and emerald eyes,
She saw; and purred applause.

Still had she gazed; but 'midst the tide
Two angel forms were seen to glide,
The Genii of the stream:
Their scaly armour's Tyrian hue
Through richest purple to the view
Betrayed a golden gleam.

The hapless Nymph with wonder saw:
A whisker first, and then a claw,
With many an ardent wish
She stretched, in vain, to reach the prize
What female heart can gold despise?
What Cat's averse to Fish?

Presumptuous maid! with looks intent
Again she stretched, again she bent,
Nor knew the gulf between—
Malignant Fate sat by, and smiled—
The slippery verge her feet beguiled;
She tumbled headlong in!

Eight times emerging from the flood
She mewed to every watery God
Some speedy aid to send:—
No Dolphin came, no Nereid stirred,
Nor cruel Tom, nor Susan heard—
A favourite has no friend!

From hence, ye Beauties, undeceived,
Know one false step is ne'er retrieved,
And be with caution bold:
Not all that tempts your wandering eyes
And heedless hearts, is lawful prize,
Nor all that glisters, gold!

THOMAS GRAY (1716-1771)

A Widow Bird

A WIDOW bird sat mourning for her love
Upon a wintry bough;
The frozen wind crept on above,
The freezing stream below.

There was no leaf upon the forest bare,
No flower upon the ground,
And little motion in the air
Except the mill-wheel's sound.

PERCY BYSSHE SHELLEY (1792-1822)

Inversnaid

THIS darksome burn, horseback brown,
His rollrock highroad roaring down,
In coop and in comb the fleece of his foam
Flutes and low to the lake falls home.

A windpuff-bonnet of fáwn-fróth
Turns and twindles over the broth
Of a pool so pitchblack, féll-frówning,
It rounds and rounds Despair to drowning.

Degged with dew, dappled with dew
Are the groins of the braes that the brook treads
through,
Wiry heathpacks, flitches of fern,
And the beadbonny ash that sits over the burn.

What would the world be, once bereft
Of wet and of wildness? Let them be left,
O let them be left, wildness and wet;
Long live the weeds and the wilderness yet.

GERARD MANLEY HOPKINS (1844-1889)

Break, Break, Break

BREAK, break, break
On thy cold gray stones, O Sea!
And I would that my tongue could utter
The thoughts that arise in me.

O, well for the fisherman's boy,
That he shouts with his sister at play!
O, well for the sailor lad,
That he sings in his boat on the bay!

And the stately ships go on
To their haven under the hill;
But O for the touch of a vanished hand,
And the sound of a voice that is still!

Break, break, break
At the foot of thy crags, O Sea!
But the tender grace of a day that is dead
Will never come back to me.

ALFRED LORD TENNYSON (1809-1892)

Out in the Dark

OUT in the dark over the snow
The fallow fawns invisible go
With the fallow doe;
And the winds blow
Fast as the stars are slow.

Stealthily the dark haunts round
And, when a lamp goes, without sound
At a swifter bound
Than the swiftest hound,
Arrives, and all else is drowned;

And I and star and wind and deer
Are in the dark together,—near,
Yet far,—and fear
Drums on my ear
In that sage company drear.

How weak and little is the light,
All the universe of sight,
Love and delight,
Before the might,
If you love it not, of night.

EDWARD THOMAS (1878-1917)

To the Moon

ART thou pale for weariness
Of climbing heaven, and gazing on the earth,
Wandering companionless
Among the stars that have a different birth,—
And ever-changing, like a joyless eye
That finds no object worth its constancy?

PERCY BYSSHE SHELLEY (1792-1822)

I Am

I AM: yet what I am none cares or knows,
My friends forsake me like a memory lost;
I am the self-consumer of my woes,
They rise and vanish in oblivious host,
Like shades in love and death's oblivion lost;
And yet I am, and live with shadows tossed

Into the nothingness of scorn and noise,
Into the living sea of waking dreams,
Where there is neither sense of life nor joys,
But the vast shipwreck of my life's esteems;
And e'en the dearest—that I loved the best—
Are strange—nay, rather stranger than the rest.

I long for scenes where man has never trod;
A place where woman never smiled or wept;
There to abide with my Creator, God,
And sleep as I in childhood sweetly slept:
Untroubling and untroubled where I lie;
The grass below—above the vaulted sky.

JOHN CLARE (1793-1864)

Even Such is Time

EVEN such is Time, that takes in trust
Our youth, our joys, and all we have,
And pays us but with age and dust;
Who in the dark and silent grave,
When we have wandered all our ways,
Shuts up the story of our days:
And from which earth, and grave, and dust,
The Lord shall raise me up, I trust.

SIR WALTER RALEIGH (?1552-1618)

The World is Too Much with Us

THE world is too much with us; late and soon,
Getting and spending, we lay waste our powers:
Little we see in Nature that is ours;
We have given our hearts away, a sordid boon!
This Sea that bares her bosom to the moon,
The winds that will be howling at all hours,
And are up-gathered now like sleeping flowers,
For this, for everything, we are out of tune;
It moves us not.—Great God! I'd rather be
A Pagan suckled in a creed outworn,
So might I, standing on this pleasant lea,
Have glimpses that would make me less forlorn;
Have sight of Proteus rising from the sea;
Or hear old Triton blow his wreathèd horn.

WILLIAM WORDSWORTH (1770-1850)

The Music-Makers

WE are the music-makers,
And we are the dreamers of dreams,
Wandering by lone sea-breakers,
And sitting by desolate streams;
World-losers and world-forsakers,
On whom the pale moon gleams:
Yet we are the movers and shakers
Of the world for ever, it seems.

With wonderful deathless ditties
We build up the world's great cities,
And out of a fabulous story
We fashion an empire's glory:
One man with a dream, at pleasure,
Shall go forth and conquer a crown;
And three with a new song's measure
Can trample an empire down.

We, in the ages lying
In the buried past of the earth,
Built Nineveh with our sighing,
And Babel itself with our mirth;
And o'erthrew them with prophesying
To the old of the new world's worth;
For each age is a dream that is dying,
Or one that is coming to birth.

ARTHUR O'SHAUGHNESSY (1844-1881)

On first looking into Chapman's Homer

MUCH have I travelled in the realms of gold
And many goodly states and kingdoms seen;
Round many western islands have I been
Which bards in fealty to Apollo hold.
Oft of one wide expanse had I been told
That deep-browed Homer ruled as his demesne;
Yet did I never breathe its pure serene
Till I heard Chapman speak out loud and bold:
Then felt I like some watcher of the skies
When a new planet swims into his ken;
Or like stout Cortez, when with eagle eyes
He stared at the Pacific—and all his men
Looked at each other with a wild surmise—
Silent, upon a peak in Darien.

JOHN KEATS (1795-1821)

A Passer-By

WHITHER, O splendid ship, thy white sails crowding,
Leaning across the bosom of the urgent West,
That fearest nor sea rising, nor sky clouding,
Whither away, fair rover, and what thy quest?
Ah! soon, when Winter has all our vales oppressed,
When skies are cold and misty, and hail is hurling,
Wilt thou glide on the blue Pacific, or rest
In a summer haven asleep, thy white sails furling.

I there before thee, in the country that well thou knowest,
Already arrived am inhaling the odorous air:
I watch thee enter unerringly where thou goest,
And anchor queen of the strange shipping there,
Thy sails for awnings spread, thy masts bare;
Nor is aught from the foaming reef to the snow-capped, grandest
Peak, that is over the feathery palms more fair
Than thou, so upright, so stately, and still thou standest.

And yet, O splendid ship, unhailed and nameless,
I know not if, aiming a fancy, I rightly divine
That thou hast a purpose joyful, a courage blameless,
Thy port assured in a happier land than mine.
But for all I have given thee, beauty enough is thine,
As thou, aslant with trim tackle and shrouding,
From the proud nostril curve of a prow's line
In the offing scatterest foam, thy white sails crowding.

ROBERT BRIDGES (1844-1930)

The Old Ships

I HAVE seen old ships sail like swans asleep
Beyond the village which men still call Tyre,
With leaden age o'ercargoed, dipping deep
For Famagusta and the hidden sun
That rings black Cyprus with a lake of fire;
And all those ships were certainly so old
Who knows how oft with squat and noisy gun,
Questing brown slaves or Syrian oranges,
The pirate Genoese
Hell-raked them till they rolled
Blood, water, fruit and corpses up the hold.
But now through friendly seas they softly run,
Painted the mid-sea blue or shore-sea green,
Still patterned with the vine and grapes in gold.

But I have seen,
Pointing her shapely shadows from the dawn
And image tumbled on a rose-swept bay,
A drowsy ship of some yet older day;
And, wonder's breath indrawn,
Thought I—who knows—who knows—but in that same
(Fished up beyond Aeaea, patched up new
—Stern painted brighter blue—)
That talkative bald-headed seaman came
(Twelve patient comrades sweating at the oar)
From Troy's doom-crimson shore,
And with great lies about his wooden horse

Set the crew laughing, and forgot his course.

It was so old a ship—who knows, who knows?
—And yet so beautiful, I watched in vain
To see the mast burst open with a rose,
And the whole deck put on its leaves again.

JAMES ELROY FLECKER (1884-1915)

A Sea Dirge

FULL fathom five thy father lies;
Of his bones are coral made:
Those are pearls that were his eyes:
Nothing of him that doth fade,
But doth suffer a sea-change
Into something rich and strange.
Sea-nymphs hourly ring his knell:
Ding-dong.
Hark! now I hear them,—ding-dong, bell.

WILLIAM SHAKESPEARE (1564-1616)
from The Tempest

Come unto these Yellow Sands

COME unto these yellow sands,
And then take hands:
Curtsied when you have, and kissed,—
The wild waves whist,—
Foot it featly here and there;
And, sweet sprites, the burden bear.
Hark, hark!
Bow-wow,
The watch-dogs bark:
Bow-wow.
Hark, hark! I hear
The strain of strutting Chanticleer
Cry, cock-a-diddle dow.

WILLIAM SHAKESPEARE (1564-1616)

Home-Thoughts, from the Sea

NOBLY, nobly Cape Saint Vincent to the North-west died away;
Sunset ran, one glorious blood-red, reeking into Cadiz Bay;
Bluish 'mid the burning water, full in face Trafalgar lay;
In the dimmest North-east distance dawned Gibraltar grand
and gray,
'Here and here did England help me: how can I help England?'
—say,
Whoso turns as I, this evening, turn to God to praise and pray,
While Jove's planet rises yonder, silent over Africa.

ROBERT BROWNING (1812-1889)

The Burial of Sir John Moore
at Corunna, 1809

NOT a drum was heard, not a funeral note,
As his corpse to the rampart we hurried;
Not a soldier discharged his farewell shot
O'er the grave where our hero we buried.

We buried him darkly, at dead of night,
The sods with our bayonets turning;
By the struggling moonbeam's misty light,
And the lantern dimly burning.

No useless coffin enclosed his breast,
Not in sheet nor in shroud we wound him;
But he lay like a warrior taking his rest,
With his martial cloak around him.

Few and short were the prayers we said,
And we spoke not a word of sorrow;
But we steadfastly gazed on the face that was dead,
And we bitterly thought of the morrow.

We thought, as we hollowed his narrow bed
And smoothed down his lonely pillow,
That the foe and the stranger would tread o'er
his head,
And we far away on the billow!
Lightly they'll talk of the spirit that's gone,
And o'er his cold ashes upbraid him;
But little he'll reck, if they let him sleep on,
In the grave where a Briton has laid him.

But half of our heavy task was done
When the clock struck the hour for retiring;
And we heard the distant and random gun
That the foe was sullenly firing.

Slowly and sadly we laid him down,
From the field of his fame fresh and gory;
We carved not a line, and we raised not a
stone—
But we left him alone with his glory.

CHARLES WOLFE (1791-1823)

Anthem for Doomed Youth

WHAT passing-bells for these who die as cattle?
Only the monstrous anger of the guns.
Only the stuttering rifles' rapid rattle
Can patter out their hasty orisons.
No mockeries now for them; no prayers nor bells,
Nor any voice of mourning save the choirs,—
The shrill, demented choirs of wailing shells;
    And bugles calling for them from sad shires.

What candles may be held to speed them all?
Not in the hands of boys, but in their eyes
Shall shine the holy glimmers of good-byes.
The pallor of girls' brows shall be their pall;
Their flowers the tenderness of patient minds,
And each slow dusk a drawing-down of blinds.

WILFRED OWEN (1893-1918)

In Time of The Breaking of Nations

ONLY a man harrowing clods
In a slow silent walk
With an old horse that stumbles and nods
Half asleep as they stalk.

Only thin smoke without flame
From the heaps of couch-grass;
Yet this will go onward the same
Though Dynasties pass.

Yonder a maid and her wight
Come whispering by:
War's annals will cloud into night
Ere their story die.

THOMAS HARDY (1840-1928)

from The Passionate Shepherd to His Love

COME live with me and be my Love,
And we will all the pleasures prove
That hills and valleys, dale and field,
And all the craggy mountains yield.

There will we sit upon the rocks
And see the shepherds feed their flocks,
By shallow rivers, to whose falls
Melodious birds sing madrigals.

There will I make thee beds of roses
And a thousand fragrant posies,
A cap of flowers, and a kirtle
Embroidered all with leaves of myrtle.

A gown made of the finest wool,
Which from our pretty lambs we pull,
Fair lined slippers for the cold,
With buckles of the purest gold …

The shepherds' swains shall dance and sing
For thy delight each May-morning:
If these delights thy mind may move,
Then live with me and be my Love.

CHRISTOPHER MARLOWE (1564-1593)

Who is Silvia?

WHO is Silvia? what is she,
That all our swains commend her?
Holy, fair, and wise is she;
The heaven such grace did lend her,
That she might admirèd be.

Is she kind as she is fair?
For beauty lives with kindness:
Love doth to her eyes repair,
To help him of his blindness;
And, being helped, inhabits there.

Then to Silvia let us sing,
That Silvia is excelling;
She excels each mortal thing
Upon the dull earth dwelling;
To her let us garlands bring.

WILLIAM SHAKESPEARE (1564-1616)
from The Two Gentlemen of Verona

from I Know Where I'm Going

I KNOW where I'm going
And I know who's going with me:
I know who I love,
But the dear knows who I'll marry.

I have stockings of silk,
Shoes of fine green leather,
Combs to buckle my hair,
And a ring for every finger.

Some say he is fine,
But I say he is bonny,
The fairest of them all,
My handsome winsome Johnny.

Feather beds are soft,
And painted rooms are bonny,
But I would leave them all
To go with my love Johnny.

I know where I'm going,
And I know who's going with me:
I know who I love,
But the dear knows who I'll marry.

ANON

Sonnet 18

SHALL I compare thee to a summer's day?
Thou art more lovely and more temperate:
Rough winds do shake the darling buds of May,
And summer's lease hath all too short a date:
Sometime too hot the eye of heaven shines,
And often is his gold complexion dimmed:
And every fair from fair sometime declines,
By chance, or nature's changing course, untrimmed.
But thy eternal summer shall not fade
Nor lose possession of that fair thou owest;
Nor shall Death brag thou wanderest in his shade,
When in eternal lines to time thou growest:
So long as men can breathe, or eyes can see,
So long lives this, and this gives life to thee.

WILLIAM SHAKESPEARE (1564-1616)

For Love's Sake

IF THOU must love me, let it be for nought
Except for love's sake only. Do not say
'I love her for her smile—her look—her way
Of speaking gently,—for a trick of thought
That falls in well with mine, and certes brought
A sense of pleasant ease on such a day'—
For these things in themselves, Beloved, may
Be changed, or change for thee,—and love, so wrought,
May be unwrought so. Neither love me for
Thine own dear pity's wiping my cheeks dry,—
Thy comfort long, and lose thy love thereby!
But love me for love's sake, that evermore
Thou mayst love on, through love's eternity.

ELIZABETH BARRETT BROWNING (1806-1861)
from Sonnets from the Portuguese

All for Love

O TALK not to me of a name great in story;
The days of our youth are the days of our glory;
And the myrtle and ivy of sweet two-and-twenty
Are worth all your laurels, though ever so plenty.

What are garlands and crowns to the brow that is wrinkled?
'Tis but as a dead flower with May-dew besprinkled:
Then away with all such from the head that is hoary—
What care I for the wreaths that can only give glory?

O Fame!—if I e'er took delight in thy praises,
'Twas less for the sake of thy high-sounding phrases,
Than to see the bright eyes of the dear one discover
She thought that I was not unworthy to love her.

There chiefly I sought thee, there only I found thee;
Her glance was the best of the rays that surround thee;
When it sparkled o'er aught that was bright in my story,
I knew it was love, and I felt it was glory.

LORD BYRON (1788-1824)

The Sick Rose

O ROSE, thou art sick!
The invisible worm
That flies in the night,
In the howling storm,

Has found out thy bed
Of crimson joy,
And his dark secret love
Does thy life destroy.

WILLIAM BLAKE (1757-1827)

A Superscription

LOOK in my face; my name is Might-have-been;
I am also called No-more, Too-late, Farewell;
Unto thine ear I hold the dead-sea shell
Cast up thy Life's foam-fretted feet between;
Unto thine eyes the glass where that is seen
Which had Life's form and Love's, but by my spell
Is now a shaken shadow intolerable,
Of ultimate things unuttered the frail screen.
Mark me, how still I am! But should there dart
One moment through thy soul the soft surprise
Of that winged Peace which lulls the breath of sighs—
Then shalt thou see me smile, and turn apart
Thy visage to mine ambush at thy heart
Sleepless with cold commemorative eyes.

DANTE GABRIEL ROSSETTI (1828-1882)

Non Sum Qualis Eram ...

LAST night, ah, yesternight, betwixt her lips and mine
There fell thy shadow, Cynara! thy breath was shed
Upon my soul between the kisses and the wine;
And I was desolate and sick of an old passion,
Yea, I was desolate and bowed my head:
I have been faithful to thee, Cynara! in my fashion.

All night upon mine heart I felt her warm heart beat,
Night-long within mine arms in love and sleep she lay;
Surely the kisses of her bought red mouth were sweet;
But I was desolate and sick of an old passion,
When I awoke and found the dawn was gray:
I have been faithful to thee, Cynara! in my fashion.

I have forgot much, Cynara! gone with the wind,
Flung roses, roses riotously with the throng,
Dancing, to put thy pale, lost lilies out of mind;
But I was desolate and sick of an old passion,
Yea, all the time, because the dance was long:
I have been faithful to thee, Cynara! in my fashion.

I cried for madder music and for stronger wine,
But when the feast is finished and the lamps expire,
Then falls thy shadow, Cynara! the night is thine;
And I am desolate and sick of an old passion,
Yea, hungry for the lips of my desire:
I have been faithful to thee, Cynara! in my fashion.

ERNEST DOWSON (1867-1900)

A Farewell

GO FETCH to me a pint o' wine,
An' fill it in a silver tassie;
That I may drink before I go
A service to my bonnie lassie:
The boat rocks at the pier o' Leith,
Fu' loud the wind blaws frae the Ferry,
The ship rides by the Berwick-law,
And I maun leave my bonnie Mary.

The trumpets sound, the banners fly,
The glittering spears are rankèd ready;
The shouts o' war are heard afar,
The battle closes thick and bloody;
But it's not the roar o' sea or shore
Wad make me langer wish to tarry;
Nor shouts o' war that's heard afar—
It's leaving thee, my bonnie Mary.

ROBERT BURNS (1759-1796)

Surprised by Joy

SURPRISED by joy—impatient as the wind—
I turned to share the transport—O with whom
But Thee—deep buried in the silent tomb,
That spot which no vicissitude can find?
Love, faithful love recalled thee to my mind—
But how could I forget thee? Through what power
Even for the least division of an hour
Have I been so beguiled as to be blind
To my most grievous loss?—That thought's return
Was the worst pang that sorrow ever bore,
Save one, one only, when I stood forlorn,
Knowing my heart's best treasure was no more;
That neither present time, nor years unborn
Could to my sight that heavenly face restore.

WILLIAM WORDSWORTH (1770-1850)

It is Not Growing Like a Tree

IT IS not growing like a tree
In bulk, doth make Man better be;
Or standing long an oak, three hundred year,
To fall a log at last, dry, bald, and sere:
A lily of a day
Is fairer far in May,
Although it fall and die that night;
It was the plant and flower of Light.
In small proportions we just beauties see;
And in short measures life may perfect be.

BEN JONSON (1572-1637)

from The Rubaiyat of Omar Khayyam

AWAKE! for Morning in the Bowl of Night
Has flung the Stone that puts the Stars to Flight:
And Lo! the Hunter of the East has caught
The Sultan's Turret in a Noose of Light.

Dreaming when Dawn's Left Hand was in the Sky
I heard a Voice within the Tavern cry,
'Awake, my Little ones, and fill the Cup
Before Life's Liquor in its Cup be dry.'

And, as the Cock crew, those who stood before
The Tavern shouted—'Open then the Door!
You know how little while we have to stay,
And, once departed, may return no more'...

Come, fill the Cup, and in the Fire of Spring
The Winter Garment of Repentance fling:
The Bird of Time has but a little way
To fly—and Lo! the Bird is on the Wing ...

Here with a Loaf of Bread beneath the Bough,
A Flask of Wine, a Book of Verse—and Thou
Beside me singing in the Wilderness—
And Wilderness is Paradise enow ...

Ah, Moon of my Delight who knowest no wane,
The Moon of Heaven is rising once again:
How oft hereafter rising shall she look
Through this same Garden after me—in vain!

And when Thyself with shining Foot shall pass
Among the Guests Star-scattered on the Grass,
And in thy joyous Errand reach the Spot
Where I made one—turn down an empty Glass!

EDWARD FITZGERALD (1809-1883)

The Pilgrim

WHO would true valour see,
Let him come hither!
One here will constant be
Come wind, come weather;
There's no discouragement
Shall make him once relent
His first-avowed intent
To be a pilgrim.

Whoso beset him round
With dismal stories,
Do but themselves confound;
His strength the more is.
No lion can him fright;
He'll with a giant fight;
He will have a right
To be a pilgrim.

Hobgoblin, nor foul fiend,
Can daunt his spirit;
He knows he at the end
Shall life inherit:—
Then, fancies fly, away;
He'll fear not what men say;
He'll labour night and day
To be a pilgrim.

JOHN BUNYAN (1628-1688)

On His Blindness

WHEN I consider how my light is spent
Ere half my days, in this dark world and wide,
And that one talent which is death to hide,
Lodged with me useless, though my soul more bent
To serve therewith my Maker, and present
My true account, lest He returning chide,—
'Doth God exact day-labour, light denied?'
I fondly ask:—But Patience to prevent
That murmur, soon replies: 'God doth not need
Either man's work, or his own gifts: who best
Bear His mild yoke, they serve Him best: His state
Is kingly: thousands at His bidding speed,
And post o'er land and ocean without rest:—
They also serve who only stand and wait.'

JOHN MILTON (1608-1674)

The Darkling Thrush

I LEANT upon a coppice gate
When Frost was spectre-gray,
And Winter's dregs made desolate
The weakening eye of day.
The tangled bine-stems scored the sky
Like strings of broken lyres,
And all mankind that haunted nigh
Had sought their household fires.

The land's sharp features seemed to be
The Century's corpse outleant,
His crypt the cloudy canopy,
The wind his death-lament.
The ancient pulse of germ and birth
Was shrunken hard and dry,
And every spirit upon earth
Seemed fervourless as I.

At once a voice arose among
The bleak twigs overhead
In a full-hearted evensong
Of joy illimited;
An aged thrush, frail, gaunt, and small,
In blast-beruffled plume,
Had chosen thus to fling his soul
Upon the growing gloom.

So little cause for carolings
Of such ecstatic sound
Was written on terrestrial things
Afar or nigh around,
That I could think there trembled through
His happy goodnight air
Some blessed Hope, whereof he knew
And I was unaware.

THOMAS HARDY (1840-1928)

Say Not, the Struggle Naught Availeth

SAY not, the struggle naught availeth,
The labour and the wounds are vain,
The enemy faints not, nor faileth,
And as things have been they remain.

If hopes were dupes, fears may be liars;
It may be, in yon smoke concealed,
Your comrades chase e'en now the fliers,
And, but for you, possess the field.

For while the tired waves, vainly breaking,
Seem here no painful inch to gain,
Far back, through creeks and inlets making,
Comes silent, flooding in, the main.

And not by eastern windows only,
When daylight comes, comes in the light,
In front, the sun climbs slow, how slowly,
But westward, look, the land is bright!

ARTHUR HUGH CLOUGH (1819-1861)

A Farewell to Arms

HIS golden locks time hath to silver turned;
O time too swift, O swiftness never ceasing!
His youth 'gainst time and age hath ever spurned
But spurned in vain, youth waneth by increasing.
Beauty, strength, youth, are flowers, but fading seen,
Duty, faith, love, are roots, and ever green.

His helmet now shall make a hive for bees,
And lovers' sonnets turned to holy psalms:
A man-at-arms must now serve on his knees,
And feed on prayers, which are age his alms.
But though from court to cottage he depart,
His saint is sure of his unspotted heart.

And when he saddest sits in homely cell,
He'll teach his swains this carol for a song:
'Blest be the hearts that wish my sovereign well,
Cursed be the souls that think her any wrong.'
Goddess, allow this aged man his right,
To be your beadsman now that was your knight.

GEORGE PEELE (1558?-1597)

from Elegy Written in a Country Churchyard

THE curfew tolls the knell of parting day,
The lowing herd winds slowly o'er the lea,
The ploughman homeward plods his weary way,
And leaves the world to darkness, and to me.

Now fades the glimmering landscape on the sight,
And all the air a solemn stillness holds,
Save where the beetle wheels his droning flight,
And drowsy tinklings lull the distant folds …

Beneath those rugged elms, that yew-tree's shade,
Where heaves the turf in many a mouldering heap,
Each in his narrow cell for ever laid,
The rude forefathers of the hamlet sleep.

The breezy call of incense-breathing morn,
The swallow twittering from the straw-built shed,
The cock's shrill clarion, or the echoing horn,
No more shall rouse them from their lowly bed …

Far from the madding crowd's ignoble strife,
Their sober wishes never learned to stray;
Along the cool sequestered vale of life
They kept the noiseless tenor of their way …

THOMAS GRAY (1716-1771)

Sparkles from the Wheel

WHERE the city's ceaseless crowd moves on the livelong day,
Withdrawn I join a group of children watching, I pause aside
with them.

By the curb toward the edge of the flagging,
A knife-grinder works at his wheel sharpening a great knife,
Bending over he carefully holds it to the stone, by foot and knee,
With measured tread he turns rapidly, as he presses with light
but firm hand,
'Forth issue then in copious golden jets,
Sparkles from the wheel.

The scene and all its belongings, how they seize and affect me,
The sad sharp-chinned old man with worn clothes and broad
shoulder-band of leather,
Myself effusing and fluid, a phantom curiously floating,
now here absorbed and arrested,
The group, (an unminded point set in a vast surrounding),
The attentive, quiet children, the loud, proud, restive base
of the streets,
The low hoarse purr of the whirling stone, the light-pressed blade,
Diffusing, dropping, sideways-darting, in tiny showers of gold,
Sparkles from the wheel.

WALT WHITMAN (1819-1892)

A Description of the Morning

NOW hardly here and there an hackney-coach
Appearing, showed the ruddy morn's approach.
Now Betty from her master's bed had flown,
And softly stole to discompose her own.
The slipshod 'prentice from his master's door
Had pared the dirt, and sprinkled round the floor.
Now Moll had whirled her mop with dexterous airs,
Prepared to scrub the entry and the stairs.
The youth with broomy stumps began to trace
The kennel edge, where wheels had worn the place.
The small-coal man was heard with cadence deep,
Till drowned in shriller notes of chimney-sweep.
Duns at his lordship's gate began to meet,
And brickdust Moll had screamed through half a street.
The turnkey now his flock returning sees,
Duly let out a-nights to steal for fees.
The watchful bailiffs take their silent stands;
And schoolboys lag with satchels in their hands.

JONATHAN SWIFT (1667-1745)

Abou Ben Adhem

ABOU Ben Adhem (may his tribe increase!)
Awoke one night from a deep dream of peace,
And saw, within the moonlight in his room,
Making it rich, and like a lily in bloom,
An angel writing in a book of gold:
Exceeding peace had made Ben Adhem bold,
And to the presence in the room he said,
'What writest thou?' The vision raised its head,
And with a look made of all sweet accord
Answered, 'The names of those who love the Lord.'
'And is mine one?' said Abou. 'Nay, not so,'
Replied the angel. Abou spoke more low,
But cheerly still; and said, 'I pray thee, then,
Write me as one that loves his fellow men.'
The angel wrote, and vanished. The next night
It came again with a great wakening light,
And showed the names whom love of God had blessed,
And lo! Ben Adhem's name led all the rest!

J H LEIGH HUNT (1784-1859)

La Belle Dame Sans Merci

O, WHAT can ail thee, knight-at-arms,
Alone and palely loitering?
The sedge has withered from the lake,
And no birds sing.

O, what can ail thee, knight-at-arms,
So haggard and so woe-begone?
The squirrel's granary is full,
And the harvest's done.

I see a lily on thy brow
With anguish moist and fever dew,
And on thy cheeks a fading rose
Fast withereth too.

I met a lady in the meads,
Full beautiful—a faery's child,
Her hair was long, her foot was light,
And her eyes were wild.

I made a garland for her head,
And bracelets too, and fragrant zone;
She looked at me as she did love,
And made sweet moan.

I set her on my pacing steed
And nothing else saw all day long,
For sidelong would she bend, and sing
A faery's song.

She found me roots of relish sweet,
And honey wild, and manna dew,
And sure in language strange she said,
'I love thee true.'

She took me to her elfin grot,
And there she wept and sighed full sore,
And there I shut her wild, wild eyes
With kisses four.

And there she lulled me asleep,
And there I dreamed—Ah! woe betide!
The latest dream I ever dreamed
On the cold hill side.

I saw pale kings and princes too,
Pale warriors, death-pale were they all:
They cried—'La belle Dame sans Merci
Hath thee in thrall!'

I saw their starved lips in the gloam
With horrid warning gaped wide,
And I awoke and found me here
On the cold hill side.

And this is why I sojourn here
Alone and palely loitering,
Though the sedge is withered from the lake,
And no birds sing.

JOHN KEATS (1795-1821)

The Sands of Dee

'O MARY, go and call the cattle home,
And call the cattle home,
And call the cattle home
Across the sands of Dee!'
The western wind was wild and dank with foam,
And all alone went she.

The western tide crept up along the sand,
And o'er and o'er the sand,
And round and round the sand,
As far as eye could see.
The rolling mist came down and hid the land:
And never home came she.

'Oh! is it weed, or fish, or floating hair—
A tress of golden hair,
A drownèd maiden's hair
Above the nets at sea?
Was never salmon yet that shone so fair
Among the stakes on Dee.'

They rowed her in across the rolling foam,
The cruel crawling foam,
The cruel hungry foam,
To her grave beside the sea:
But still the boatmen hear her call the cattle home
Across the sands of Dee.

CHARLES KINGSLEY (1819-1875)

Ah, Sunflower!

AH, SUNFLOWER! weary of time,
Who countest the steps of the sun,
Seeking after that sweet golden clime
Where the traveller's journey is done:

Where the youth pined away with desire,
And the pale virgin shrouded in snow
Arise from their graves, and aspire
Where my sunflower wishes to go.

WILLIAM BLAKE (1757-1827)

Vitae Summa Brevis Spem Nos Vetat Incohare Longam

THEY are not long, the weeping and the laughter,
Love and desire and hate:
I think they have no portion in us after
We pass the gate.

They are not long, the days of wine and roses:
Out of a misty dream
Our path emerges for a while, then closes
Within a dream.

ERNEST DOWSON (1867-1900)

from The Garden of Proserpine

HERE, where the world is quiet;
Here, where all trouble seems
Dead winds' and spent waves' riot
In doubtful dreams of dreams;
I watch the green field growing
For reaping folk and sowing,
For harvest-time and mowing,
A sleepy world of streams.

I am tired of tears and laughter,
And men that laugh and weep;
Of what may come hereafter
For men that sow to reap:
I am weary of days and hours,
Blown buds of barren flowers,
Desires and dreams and powers
And everything but sleep ...

From too much love of living,
From hope and fear set free,
We thank with brief thanksgiving
Whatever gods may be
That no life lives for ever;
That dead men rise up never;
That even the weariest river
Winds somewhere safe to sea ...

A C SWINBURNE (1837-1909)

Dream-Pedlary

IF THERE were dreams to sell,
What would you buy?
Some cost a passing bell;
Some a light sigh,
That shakes from Life's fresh crown
Only a rose-leaf down.
If there were dreams to sell,
Merry and sad to tell,
And the crier rung the bell,
What would you buy?

A cottage lone and still,
With bowers nigh,
Shadowy, my woes to still,
Until I die.
Such pearl from Life's fresh crown
Fain would I shake me down.
Were dreams to have at will,
This would best heal my ill,
This would I buy.

But there were dreams to sell
Ill didst thou buy;
Life is a dream, they tell,
Waking, to die.
Dreaming a dream to prize,

Is wishing ghosts to rise:
And, if I had the spell
To call the buried well,
Which one would I?

If there are ghosts to raise,
What shall I call,
Out of hell's murky haze,
Heaven's blue pall?
Raise my loved long-lost boy
To lead me to his joy.
There are no ghosts to raise;
Out of death lead no ways;
Vain is the call.

Know'st thou not ghosts to sue?
No love thou hast.
Else lie, as I will do,
And breathe thy last.
So out of Life's fresh crown
Fall like a rose-leaf down.
Thus are the ghosts to woo;
Thus are all dreams made true,
Ever to last!

THOMAS LOVELL BEDDOES (1803-1849)

Up-Hill

DOES the road wind up-hill all the way?
Yes, to the very end.
Will the day's journey take the whole long day?
From morn to night, my friend.

But is there for the night a resting-place?
A roof for when the slow dark hours begin.
May not the darkness hide it from my face?
You cannot miss that inn.

Shall I meet other wayfarers at night?
Those who have gone before.
Then must I knock, or call when just in sight?
They will not keep you standing at that door.

Shall I find comfort, travel-sore and weak?
Of labour you shall find the sum.
Will there be beds for me and all who seek?
Yea, beds for all who come.

CHRISTINA ROSSETTI (1830-1894)

A Slumber Did My Spirit Seal

A SLUMBER did my spirit seal;
I had no human fears:
She seemed a thing that could not feel
The touch of earthly years.

No motion has she now, no force;
She neither hears nor sees;
Rolled round in earth's diurnal course
With rocks, and stones, and trees.

WILLIAM WORDSWORTH (1770-1850)

Epitaph

UNDER the wide and starry sky
Dig the grave and let me lie:
Glad did I live and gladly die,
And I laid me down with a will.

This be the verse you grave for me:
Here he lies where he longed to be;
Home is the sailor, home from sea,
And the hunter home from the hill.

ROBERT LOUIS STEVENSON (1850-1894)

Tintern Abbey

FIVE years have past; five summers, with the length
Of five long winters! and again I hear
These waters, rolling from their mountain-springs
With a soft inland murmur.—Once again
Do I behold these steep and lofty cliffs,
That on a wild secluded scene impress
Thoughts of more deep seclusion; and connect
The landscape with the quiet of the sky.
The day is come when I again repose
Here, under this dark sycamore, and view
These plots of cottage-ground, these orchard-tufts,
Which at this season, with their unripe fruits,
Are clad in one green hue, and lose themselves
'Mid groves and copses. Once again I see
These hedge-rows, hardly hedge-rows, little lines
Of sportive wood run wild: these pastoral farms,
Green to the very door; and wreaths of smoke
Sent up, in silence, from among the trees! …

For I have learned
To look on nature, not as in the hour
Of thoughtless youth; but hearing oftentimes
The still, sad music of humanity,
Nor harsh nor grating, though of ample power

To chasten and subdue. And I have felt
A presence that disturbs me with the joy
Of elevated thoughts; a sense sublime
Of something far more deeply interfused,
Whose dwelling is the light of setting suns,
And the round ocean and the living air,
And the blue sky, and in the mind of man:
A motion and a spirit, that impels
All thinking things, all objects of all thought,
And rolls through all things. Therefore am I still
A lover of the meadows and the woods,
And mountains; and of all that we behold
From this green earth; of all the mighty world
Of eye, and ear,—both what they half create,
And what perceive; well pleased to recognise
In nature and the language of the sense
The anchor of my purest thoughts, the nurse,
The guide, the guardian of my heart, and soul
Of all my moral being …

WILLIAM WORDSWORTH (1770-1850)
from Lines composed a few miles above Tintern
Abbey, on revisiting the banks of the Wye
during a tour. July 13, 1798.

Upon Westminster Bridge

EARTH has not anything to show more fair:
Dull would he be of soul who could pass by
A sight so touching in its majesty:
This City now doth like a garment wear
The beauty of the morning: silent, bare,
Ships, towers, domes, theatres, and temples lie
Open unto the fields, and to the sky,
All bright and glittering in the smokeless air.
Never did sun more beautifully steep
In his first splendour valley, rock, or hill;
Ne'er saw I, never felt, a calm so deep!
The river glideth at his own sweet will:
Dear God! the very houses seem asleep;
And all that mighty heart is lying still!

WILLIAM WORDSWORTH (1770-1850)

The Windhover: To Christ Our Lord

I CAUGHT this morning morning's minion, kingdom of
daylight's dauphin, dapple-dawn-drawn Falcon, in his riding
Of the rolling level underneath him steady air, and striding
High there, how he rung upon the rein of a wimpling wing
In his ecstasy! then off, off forth on swing,
As a skate's heel sweeps smooth on a bow-bend: the hurl and
gliding
Rebuffed the big wind. My heart in hiding
Stirred for a bird,—the achieve of, the mastery of the thing!

Brute beauty and valour and act, oh, air, pride, plume, here
Buckle! AND the fire that breaks from thee then, a billion
Times told lovelier, more dangerous, O my chevalier!

No wonder of it: shéer plód makes plough down sillion
Shine, and blue-bleak embers, ah my dear,
Fall, gall themselves, and gash gold-vermilion.

GERARD MANLEY HOPKINS (1844-1889)

The World's Wanderers

TELL me, thou Star, whose wings of light
Speed thee in thy fiery flight,
In what cavern of the night
Will thy pinions close now?

Tell me, Moon, thou pale and gray
Pilgrim of Heaven's homeless way,
In what depth of night or day
Seekest thou repose now?

Weary Wind, who wanderest
Like the world's rejected guest,
Hast thou still some secret nest
On the tree or billow?

PERCY BYSSHE SHELLEY (1792-1822)

On the Beach at Night Alone

ON the beach at night alone,
As the old mother sways her to and fro, singing her husky song,
As I watch the bright stars shining, I think a thought of the clef of
the universes, and of the future.

A vast similitude interlocks all,
All spheres, grown, ungrown, small, large, suns, moons,
planets, comets, asteroids,
All the substances of the same, and all that is spiritual upon
the same,
All distances of place, however wide,
All distances of time—all inanimate forms,
All Souls—all living bodies, though they be ever so different,
or in different worlds,
All gaseous, watery, vegetable, mineral processes—the fishes,
the brutes,
All men and women—me also;
All nations, colours, barbarisms, civilisations, languages;
All identities that have existed, or may exist, on this globe, or
any globe;
All lives and deaths—all of the past, present, future;
This vast similitude spans them, and always has spanned, and
shall forever span them, and compactly hold them, and
enclose them.

WALT WHITMAN (1819-1892)

The Everlasting Hills

HIGH among the lonely hills,
While I lay beside my sheep,
Rest came down and filled my soul,
From the everlasting deep.

Changeless march the stars above,
Changeless morn succeeds to even;
Still the everlasting hills,
Changeless watch the changeless heaven ...

CHARLES KINGSLEY (1819-1875)
From The Saint's Tragedy

The Starlight Night

LOOK at the stars! look, look up at the skies!
O look at all the fire-folk sitting in the air!
The bright boroughs, the circle-citadels there!
Down in dim woods the diamond delves! the elves'-eyes!
The grey lawns cold where gold, where quickgold lies!
Wind-beat whitebeam! airy abeles set on a flare!
Flake-doves sent floating forth at a farmyard scare!—
Ah well! it is all a purchase, all is a prize.
Buy then! bid then!—What?—Prayer, patience, alms, vows.
Look, look: a May-mess, like on orchard boughs!
Look! March-bloom, like on mealed-with-yellow sallows!
These are indeed the barn; withindoors house
The shocks. This piece-bright paling shuts the spouse
Christ home, Christ and his mother and all his hallows.

GERARD MANLEY HOPKINS (1844-1889)

How Sweet the Moonlight Sleeps

HOW sweet the moonlight sleeps upon this bank!
Here will we sit, and let the sounds of music
Creep in our ears: soft stillness and the night
Become the touches of sweet harmony.
Sit, Jessica: look, how the floor of heaven
Is thick inlaid with patines of bright gold:
There's not the smallest orb which thou behold'st
But in his motion like an angel sings,
Still quiring to the young-eyed cherubins;
Such harmony is in immortal souls.

WILLIAM SHAKESPEARE (1564-1616)
from The Merchant of Venice

Our Revels Now Are Ended

Our revels now are ended. These our actors
As I foretold you, were all spirits and
Are melted into air, into thin air:
And, like the baseless fabric of this vision,
The cloud-capped towers, the gorgeous palaces,
The solemn temples, the great globe itself,
Yea, all which it inherit, shall dissolve,
And, like this insubstantial pageant faded,
Leave not a rack behind. We are such stuff
As dreams are made on, and our little life
Is rounded with a sleep.

WILLIAM SHAKESPEARE (1564-1616)
from The Tempest